Of Heads & Hearts

ALSO BY LUCY HAMILTON

Sonnets for my Mother (Hearing Eye, 2009)
Stalker (Shearsman Books, 2012)

Lucy Hamilton

Of Heads & Hearts

Shearsman Books

First published in the United Kingdom in 2018 by
Shearsman Books
50 Westons Hill Drive
Emersons Green
BRISTOL
BS16 7DF

Shearsman Books Ltd Registered Office
30–31 St. James Place, Mangotsfield, Bristol BS16 9JB
(this address not for correspondence)

www.shearsman.com

ISBN 978-1-84861-571-7

ACKNOWLEDGEMENTS

Thanks are due to the editors of the following magazines in which many of
these poems, or earlier versions of them, first appeared: *Shearsman, PN Review,
Molly Bloom, Litmus, Her Wings of Glass Anthology, Tears in the Fence,
The Wolf* and *The Rialto*. A group of poems from 'The Diarists' appeared in
PN Review 220 and in an exhibition at The Scott Polar Research Institute,
Cambridge, for which I am grateful to Michael Schmidt, Heather Lane,
Naomi Boneham, Rosie Amos and Joseph Minden.

My thanks to Mimi Khalvati, Kaddy Benyon, Lucy Sheerman,
Joanne Limburg, Peter Collier, Clare Crossman, Jeri Onitskansky,
Fiona Moore, Hannah Lowe, Ali Thurm, Joanna Clark, Linda Black,
Jan Kofi-Tsekpo and Jude Rosen. Thanks also to Tony Frazer.

I wish to thank James and Mary Yardley, mutual friends of the 'Engineer',
for their extended friendship and kindness.

Special thanks to the real-life protagonists of these poems
for their generosity and permissions.

CONTENTS

Section I

Geometries & Numbers   11
Wigs & Dyes   12
Codes & Folios   13
Orthogonals & Transversals   14
Wild Sage & Camomile   15
Rice & Wine   16
Mules & Men   17
Tati the Parrot   18
Nostalgia & Goose-bumps   19
The Biblioteca Wittockiana   20
Murders & Mourning   21
Fossils & Manga   22
Rhymes & Riddles   23

Section II: The Diarists

Pictures & Frames   27
Letters & Diaries   28
Bells & Thimbles   29
Ice & Tears   30
Penguin & Lamb   31
Aches & Pains   32
Glaciers & Robins   33
Small Differences in the Spectrum of Black   34
De Incidentibus in Fluido / Hecest Horrenda Caribdis 35
Crocodiles & Frigate Birds   36
Notes & Quotes   37
Bedtime Stories   38
Papuan Canoes & Items (Property of
       the Royal Geographical Society)
              Lost Overboard   39
The Diarist's Dressing Up Box   40

Section III

Flags & Headbands   43
Women & Men   44
Heads & Hats   45
Black Tie & Jacket   46
Donkeys & Dreams   47
Apitherapy   48
Glockenspiel & Cymbals   49
Football & Flu   50
Cycles & Wheels   51
L'Ochju di Santa Lucia   52
Bells & Minarets   53
Grey Squirrels & Egyptian Geese   54
Nomads & Love Quests   55
Out-of-Roundness & Thin-walled Cylinders   56

Section IV: Requiem for the Engineer

Blood Letting (I-IV)   61
Soil & Grit   63
Sage & Water   64
Body & Wings   65
Crossbill & Fruit   66
Collaging the Bohemian Angels   67
Impact Under Pressure (I)   69
Impact Under Pressure (II)   70
Impact Under Pressure (III)   71
Impact Under Pressure (IV)   72
Impact Under Pressure (V)   73
Impact Under Pressure (VI)   74

Section V

Rings & Circles   77

Notes   79

For my family and friends
who inspired these poems

With love & admiration

I

Geometries & Numbers

The Polymath is sitting at the white round table drawing tangents with his protractor, set-square, ruler and compass. The Art Dealer hovers by hoping against hope that the proportional measurements between the 'dots' on his bronze insignia, a stylised representation of a symmetric 8-petal flower, match those of the Rosette in Milan Cathedral. The wall is covered in the Polymath's chalk equations, diagrams and formulae. I'm planning to paper another with his beautiful pen & ink diagrams. He frequently achieves an almost complete model but there's always one essential component that refuses to fit and I tell him it's like doing the Rubik's Cube. On a dresser next to the old Dutch wood-burner there's a wooden ship he bought me from a tea plantation in Java. We seldom drink *tea* in Spyglass Inn and when we dance on the boards and hear a thuc everyone cries *There goes the ship!* Yes, a frieze of bright-inked diamonds, cubes, rectangles and triangles and from the ceiling octahedra and tetrahedra flying around like Chinese kites.

Wigs & Dyes

E very day the Entrepreneur flits from place to place wearing *Mary May*, like a humming bird flaunting its blond & crimson feathers. Her office is crowded with *Babu / Nikki / Alex / Abdul / Oska / Aziza / Britney / Molly / Minka* – for nowadays as in ancient Egypt both genders wear wigs. Back then heads were shaved and embellished with wigs threaded from sheep's wool or vegetable fibres dyed in inks from plants, oak-bark & shellfish – to protect against sunstroke or lice-infestation. Ever since people could create they've been adding pigment to the world around them. The Entrepreneur is no exception. While Egyptian queens adorn their wigs with ornaments of gold & ivory, she loops ribbons in *Mary May*, and on her bike festooned with plastic flowers brightens the city where ever she goes.

Codes & Folios

The Art Dealer is collecting citations from the most ancient texts – the *Dead Sea Scrolls* and the *Codex Sinaiticus*: the solar and lunar week, lunations and weekday dates, monthly and yearly cycles from Babylonia and Egypt which the ancients used as mnemo-technique to teach computation of reliable religious festivals. The folios are stretched skin of donkey or antelope and it's thought 360 animals were slaughtered for the *Codex*. He's trawling for Jewish and Christian references before turning to the Arabic sources. He has produced eighteen Word pages – about six thousand words itching in his fingertips. Outside of this writing process he's forever 'losing marbles', as though his brain-box had shifted to another zone throwing an entirely new and stretched perspective on the world.

Orthogonals & Transversals

The Architect is working on a painting overlooking the Tarn, which he started during his annual painting trip to France. He's enraptured by the pink brick of Albi Cathedral blazing like a rose in the Midi sun. He sighs, twiddles his chubby fingers and sips his pint of Adnams. Today has not gone well. Years enslaved by perspective and a prodigious memory! He's Theseus in a labyrinth of orthogonals & transversals whose Ariadne has snapped the thread of the ball she is spinning. The Polymath suggests a trip to the Blue Ball at Grantchester.

Shifting his pint, the Architect spreads the photos of his paintings. It's a tour of aqueducts & amphitheatres, rock-faces, gorges, castles & cathedrals. I search for his faithless Ariadne, willing her to emerge from a glint of river, a spiral cloud, a flash of red hibiscus. I ask about the recent commission. Finished, he says cheerfully. The Royal Scot steaming on Platform 2, the commissioner's father – tam o'shanter & hackle cocked at a jaunty angle: Royal Scots Fusiliers, 1st Battalion. And I know that everything is to scale – meticulous and flawless.

Wild Sage & Camomile

The Engineer is applying to be Director of Corsican Railways, as advertised in *Corse Matin*. A dream come true for a structural & material engineer with a good track record. The perfect post for a foreigner with a fresh perspective. She's attempting transmigration, speaking the *lingua corsa*, flitting between Cambridge & Calvi according to season & pocket. The washing-machine's been fixed and she's planted two vines & three trees: apricot, grapefruit & olive, along with the desert scrub *lantana* – the name of her parents' house in Liverpool. The little garden is a repository for wild sage & camomile and her cooking-pot is varied & generous. She brings her once-eminent father here to nurture him through dementia. But he refuses to eat, wanders the streets, and before the year's through he's transported back to Liverpool.

Rice & Wine

On the pine worktop clean cooking implements lie in parallels. Garlicky knives, forks & spoons are cross-layered in neat little stacks. At each extreme of the work-surface a white teacup brims with rice. A bottle of red glints at the ready. As he stirs & tastes the sticky *Oriza sativa*, the Polymath recalls water-buffalo working straight lines across the paddy fields. The men plough while the women plant seedlings, half-hidden under wide-brimmed hats – just like the carvings in the Prambanan temples! There's jasmine tea and red or white Brema distilled from black & white rice. When he brings the *nasi goreng* to the table, I'm dancing with the Architect. The Javanese ship wobbles on the shelf above the fire.

Mules & Men

The Diarist has inadvertently deleted her latest draft. The story's imagined but she knows it well, easily retrieving Tangiers: the noise & mules & men excitingly shocking to the 1930s English! Oranges, grapefruit & lemons spilling from the trees and how she'd insisted on the trip, travelling alone to join her man at work and now these two small boys enter the script. Her daughter helps research dockers, ratchets & abduction ... *In a raid against Lisbon in 1189, the Almohad caliph Yaqub al-Mansur took 3,000 female and child captives to the Atlas Mountains.* And here are Mohammed & Hassan stowed in a Moroccan container, turning up on a Felixstowe truck, searching for their blood mother.

Tati the Parrot

The Polymath is creating a model to demonstrate analogies of space and time across physical and biological structures. He nurtures it in his head and in the diagrams he draws with coloured pens – calculations a cosmologist transfers into Euclidian graphics. Meanwhile the Art Dealer is asking him questions about Pythagoras and the pattern of 3 in the rosette windows of Milan Cathedral, adding that 52 is the number he found in a book about the Dome of the Rock in Jerusalem where a medieval Arab traveller witnessed a liturgy being performed. Today and every day at the appointed hour 52 *lascars* anoint the tip of the Rock with sweet-smelling ointments. And because his hotel window looks down on a second-hand bookshop in Zurich he slips out and buys *Tales of Tati the Parrot* who whispers, in attentive ears only, 52 moral/behavioural injunctions. I say it must be the same parrot that flew into John Ashbery's *L'Heure Exquise*. Then he tells us that a medieval numerologist may for a fee like 3 hen's eggs or a bushel of barley, inform you that the number 5, compounded with a Pythagorean triangle, mutates into the Octagon which supports the Dome of the Heavens.

Nostalgia & Goose-bumps

The Diarist has had another fall. A black bruise is spreading from wrist to elbow which she says looks worse than it is. She tends her garden from the scooter, plucking weeds with long tweezers. Men are repairing the little stream's bank and mallards waddle up to the door. *Nostalgia might find a place ...* and as she talks my skin prickles with goose-bumps. She was five years old, brother four, sister two. And to think it was an undergraduate at King's College Cambridge! She lends me her late brother's book and night after night I glimpse the murdered father they barely knew: explorer, doctor, botanist, entomologist collecting nepenthes & aromatic balsams, treating malaria & beri-beri, discovering a tribe of *very small, very jolly* Dyaks.

The Biblioteca Wittockiana

The diagram on vellum is in the form of a 36-petal flower, each of the petal's 10 calendar days attributed in Latin or Gaelic. It is placed like the incipit on a Latin calendar from Christ's Church at Canterbury and the roughly cubic shape inside the circle is plastered all over Iranian mosques. This reminds me of the Polymath's diagrams: vertices, faces, edges of cubes and octahedra; a smaller octahedron inside a cube so all its vertices touch the centre of each cube-face. *It's time to be Zen*, says the Art Dealer. *Time to tend the garden at your feet with Voltaire's recipe for serenity.* And today he attends the 25th Anniversary Opening of the Library and meets the author of *Humanists and Bookbindings of the 15th and 16th Centuries*. Now he's postulating that the design symbolises something that transcends religious divisions, that the calendar fits a time when Sufis, Humanists and Jews were striving to strip the bloody edges off creeds.

Murders & Mourning

The September victims are all young. Shot with Kalashnikovs according to *Corse Matin*. Now in Calvi another man is gunned down – *an ex-convict with blood on his hands*. The Engineer posts a recording of *Pie Jesu* on Facebook – from Fauré's *Requiem*. She sang it at her mother's funeral last year and writes: 'Almost all the most precious moments in my life have come about due to singing, or other musical occasions.' Seventeen unoccupied holiday homes are blown up and the police say these are mafia-style vendettas. But the word 'requiem' of *Sempiternam requiem* has a gentle upward upward motion.

Fossils & Manga

The Entrepreneur gift-wraps eighty gingerbread Santas and donates them to the Cancer Help Centre, where every Wednesday she works as a volunteer. But the following day, responding to a message on her blog, she cycles back there with all the boy-styles. Sam's chemo for leukaemia has made all his hair fall out but he wouldn't be seen dead in an NHS freebie. He's done his homework and has witnessed the past in jars – the fossilized example of *osteo sarcoma* in a prehistoric man, the rare tumour on the face of a little Chilean girl who lived and played sometime between 300-600A.D. Sam grabs his moment. He merges his PET scans into his visual art, imaging his body in primary colours. Now all he needs is hair. He tries on *Toni, Babu, Oska, & Ryuu* before settling for *Katsu* – black Manga boy-wig streaked with Tyrian purple.

Rhymes & Riddles

The Diarist is working with fragments. After nearly nine decades she finds them closer to the surface. (The bruise from the tooth-extraction is fading.) She can't piece together or compose a rhyme without reason. (She will get a second opinion about all this root-canal treatment.) There is no answer. The fundamental question will remain a riddle. The idea/& or irony that during the English Civil War *Humpty Dumpty* was a powerful cannon does not concern her. *The question is,* said Alice, *whether you can make words mean so many different things.* She'll raise the witnesses and give each his perspective. Each her voice. *Impenetrability! That's what I say!* And Humpty is right. *WHY?* is for ever her little brother's anguished cry. (She can't sit with her mouth clamped open for ninety minutes!) There's a question she has finally been able to formulate. It will not find closure, no, but to raise the question ... to consider the issue of *forgiveness* ... is that not something?

II

The Diarists

for Georgina Thompson

Pictures & Frames

The Diarist is writing a century after the Expeditions. She is not famous but is courageous & resolute, delving deep, excavating through layers of memory and silted-up grief. She is trying to form a greater picture, framing the two explorers in a diptych as they set off in the same year, same century. Unlike the men, she has achieved a venerable store of years. She wants to shift her obsession to theirs just as *Pennel 'swung' the ship for compass adjustment* – to absorb herself in their joys & trials until the end, so her pain becomes theirs and so their acceptance and grace – *I ought not to complain, but it is hard to be philosophic* – becoming hers, might deepen into … no, not closure – into a kind of forgiveness.

Letters & Diaries

She will call them Capt. S. & Dr. S. she thinks, making a list, wryly noting the absurdity of her (Tesco) inventory alongside theirs as she fixes her stick & bag on the scooter that's a sledge without huskies, thinking her cleaner will bring in the goods like a Sherpa. She too has a team – daughters & sons & grandchildren, a nurse bandaging the ulcerated leg in the comfort of … oh to think of the frost-bite in that tent, to contemplate the swamps, the malaria & beri-beri – but where to start, how to sort & sift & record? She must re-read the letters & diaries as her strength & sight allow – make lists, keep a journal of scraps & fragments, positioning the magnifying-glass to bring it all closer, amplifying the past in small stages.

Bells & Thimbles

Naturally it's the two doctors who intrigue her most, are closest to her heart, having so much on their top-soil so to speak, as tangible in scientific approach – the notes & sketches – as the violets & begonias on her patio. Of course the flower named after Dr. S. was a primula – *It has four to six bells on each stem, the size of a lady's thimble, of deep blue colour and lined inside with frosted silver.* And didn't her daughter say it's exquisitely rare and available on the internet from specialist nurseries? It's in her brother's book – *Primula wollanstonii* – her poor dead brother. Yes, that's the connection with Capt. S! *His* tragic death left a son aged three-and-a-half ... same age as her brother when their father ... when Dr. S. perished. That kind of correlation penetrates to the bitterest roots ... *racine: lien solide qui donne de la stabilité.*

Ice & Tears

Here is a man who knows he is going to die. *The boy will be your comfort I had looked forward to helping you to bring him up but he it is a satisfaction to feel that he is safe with you ...* and the Diarist flicks to the photograph, envisaging the frost-bitten lips, those final moments in the tent with his two surviving companions. Dr. S. on the other hand, snatched away in a freak coincidence: a policeman knocking on the Fellow's door, where the student, the brilliant but now psychotic student – *adj. recorded 1910* – opened fire on them all. She leans over the magnifying-glass, moved almost to tears by the quoted words she knows so well ... *Of this tragedy, with its waste and misery, I can neither write nor speak.*

Penguin & Lamb

As material accumulates – letters, diaries, books – the Diarist works obsessively, scribbling lists on bills, envelopes, even prescriptions, gathering piles. She alights on words, sucked in, mesmerised, begins to type in 24 pt. – *The dogs sit with their tails to this invading water, their coats wet and dripping* ... picturing her daughter's lurcher Qin shaking himself with glee, water spraying, children shrieking ... *It is a pathetic attitude, deeply significant of cold and misery; occasionally some poor beast emits a long whine.* It's one thing to keep dogs at the South Pole but on a ship in mountainous seas? *The group forms a picture of wretched dejection; such a life is truly hard for these poor creatures.*

She flicks through the book, weak eyes scrutinising passages highlighted yellow, then turns to her Kindle, the letters so big it's painfully slow: *Sunday, December 25, Christmas Day. – A merry evening just concluded.* What larks! Preparing Christmas with her younger daughter, the whole family about to arrive – not for *an excellent dinner: tomato soup, penguin breast stewed as an entrée* – but where's the lamb ... the 2 kilo newly roasted? Qin in the sitting-room, haunches up, tucking in, then slouching away grinning, oh shameless! tail wagging. She and her daughter in hysterics as they cut out the teeth marks.

Aches & Pains

*L*et food be your medicine says Hippocrates and it's true that the
Diarist suffered no spongy gums on the farm – rations notwith-
standing. She will get a second opinion about all this root-canal
treatment, she thinks, examining photos of Dr. S: *There are no vegetables,
and – what is more necessary in these places where one's appetite is poor – no
variety.* Today's young have it on a plate. The two hailed on BBC News
… Ben something … in Antarctica … and his Norwegian friend Tarka.
Capt. S. on the other hand received bad press. Some said the acerbic
comments about colleagues – *there is just a small want of precision in his
arguments* – reveal aspects of his censorious character. No, no, she can't
sit with her mouth clamped open for ninety minutes!

Glaciers & Robins

Dante was right when he placed the circles of ice below the circles of fire.
Apsley Cherry-Garrard

*T*he terrifying ice-cliffs are always changing, writes the Diarist, con-
stantly repelling and attracting. How did they survive the long
winter? Did they quarrel? Yes sir, damn you sir. This morning,
sitting outside on her scooter, she'd begun to pull ivy from the primroses
when the robin arrived like a spirit into the tiny world – so close she
could see its black eye. She studies the photo: *I hate the way we seem so
small in the menacing vastness, pulled down to unspeakable depths.* Those
who'd returned like Cherry-Garrard were never the same. Yes, and then
suddenly her scooter had shifted, tilted, and was rolling down the bank
towards the stream. And there she was, inches from the water, grappling
for her phone as the image of poor Cherry flashed into her mind, swing-
ing in his harness above the dark void.

Small Differences in the Spectrum of Black

Trapped again, thinks the Diarist, lying face-down and hurt, breathing fast & shallow. How suddenly a safe space changes to constriction. How quickly a small Eden transforms. Those photos she scrutinised ... the aerial view from a satellite image – scientists using a multispectrum radiometer to infer green from infra-red, vegetation of country A to country B – right down to the field work, close to the ground. Centipedes & ants busy in their forest by her hand ... *And he gave it for his opinion that whoever could make two ears of corn or two blades of grass to grow ...*

And what was Cherry thinking as he swung in the dark crevasse? Of the distinction between colours of ice? Small differences in the spectrum of black? Did he think of his mother? And did a garden robin cause her to start, heart in her mouth? The Diarist's own robin ... that phone-call. Oh she would ... sooner than re-live ... H in the Yemen supervising damage limitation from the oil fields, checking water in the village pump. Suddenly snatched, hooded & trussed. Within a few minutes his wide-walking space shrivelled and the blazing sun was eclipsed.

De Incidentibus in Fluido / Hecest Horrenda Caribdis

After Victor Hugo & Edgar Allan Poe

The Diarist presses a button, luxuriating in the rising hot water as her body submerges. She lies back, folding her long legs like a dragonfly. Steam and fatigue wash over her and she closes her eyes. Voices waft through the open window. Laughter. Infectious laughter. Raucous, menacing laughter louder & louder and she gasps as she rises high against a rotor wall, instinctively spreading her limbs in cruciform. Faster & faster she spins, eyes wide – not shut tight like her father's and siblings' – as grisly scenes flash by. A fat man riding a beer barrel with a huge meat pie on his head. A procession of lepers. A mountebank dressed in bearskins. A young boy, his face mutilated, mouth carved into a perpetual grin. The laughter swells into a tremendous upsurge.

She is pinned to a wall of water like a drenched butterfly. The noise is deafening and she screams as she drops into a belt of surf spinning round with terrifying velocity. Now the wall rises sheer above her – a towering black mountainous ridge of water. Round & round she is swept in swings & jerks, slowly progressing downward at each revolution. She's not alone. Her father's below, two younger siblings above. A barrel judders nearby. A monster-serpent coils into view, a four-masted ship crushed in its grip … *Beyond the shadow of the ship, I watched the water-snakes.* A whale heaves by, the orcus attacking it still attached. With a sickening heart she watches her father fasten himself to the ship, and after a couple of wild gyrations sees it plunge headlong into the foaming abyss. And now a great change takes place.

Crocodiles & Frigate Birds

I t's years since the Diarist last saw it. Men had to manoeuvre it *[one good tree & axe for hollowing]* through trap-doors up to the third floor, winch it upon ceiling-rollers in two, or was it three, pieces? It's the only object of his on display in the museum *[long planks from single tree]*, one small notice with his name and the year of the Expedition. No items of clothing *[pieces of rattan]*, no diaries or sophisticated instruments. When they were small her awestruck children fingered its intricate crocodile *[carved beast for figurehead]* and frigate birds in perpetual flight: now the canoe is suspended so high you can't see inside *[wooden weights, hooks, scrapers, thwarts, brackets]*. Last night they all crowded round, skyping a granddaughter in Bolivia. And she could see her face and hear her voice. It's amazing what one little 'periscope' can do.

Notes & Quotes

The Diarist's son owns a fibreglass sports kayak. When he goes. When he goes white-water kayaking in the Atlas Mountains. Only a Greenlandic kayak is called *qajaq*. C's kayak would be *qajariaq* meaning 'like a *qajaq*'. Each man's *qajaq* is built to the specifications of his body. *I always tried to make it so that it was not too short – so that I could load the insides with skins and provisions.* The Inuit copy the animals – that ivory bear Uncle Tom sent for her 10th birthday! – wear the skins on corresponding parts of their bodies. The women sew a seal-gut jacket – *tuilik* – with a bone-needle in two-layered leather stitching so as not to hole the fabric, to retain water-tightness. C. wears his neoprene wetsuit & jacket. When he goes white-water kayaking on the Oued Ouzoud. When he wears his fibre-glass crash helmet. When he plunges between rockfaces. Flies between water & sky.

Bedtime Stories

I

And the Diarist smiles, seeing as vividly as yesterday their eager little faces pleading to hear Grandfather again & again: *In the worst and deepest of the rapids, we touched a sunken tree, upset, and the canoe went careering bottom up down the stream.* The father she hardly knew ... *I got caught in some of the underwater branches of the tree, was dragged deep down to where it was horrible and quite dark* ... How still they lay and rapt, eyes wide as owls'. Oh, the times he escaped by a feather! *I was carried along by the current at a hideous pace towards another swift and deep rapid ... which would certainly have been the end of me, had the Dyak not caught sight* ... The children learning to swim & sail.

II

Not a day goes by that she doesn't think of Mother. Mother who was 'waiting until you were old enough to understand'. Standing at the fireplace, turning her face away to tell what her brother already knew – but he hadn't believed the boy at school. Now it was true. He would never forgive. Not until she'd persuade him to write his own book ... *Ironically Dr. S. became better known for his appalling death than for his distinguished life.* Mother on the stairs trying to hide her tears ... *For us she published a selection of his letters & diaries.* Now it's the grandchildren reading *The canoe was recovered, but the sack containing my bedding and everything else was lost.*

Papuan Canoes & Items (Property of the Royal Geographical Society) Lost Overboard

Sapoerantan   [Sweeper of the Reaches] | prismatic compass & old
                                                                silver encas₀

Bordjang Baleh   [Return of the Bachelor] | Sanderson camera   &
                                                                December diar₀

Bordjang Kilat   [The Flash of Lightning] | Zeiss telephoto lens &
                                                                six dark slide₀

Makan Tandjong [The Eater of the Bends] | Congo medicine-chest* &
                                                                beddin₀

*Used on Shackleton's Antarctic Expedition

The Diarist's Dressing Up Box

Pair of suede boots

>   *Mother had worn them in the Andes, when she was first married. We
>   loved these boots with the stiff laces up the front.*

Two red velvet coronets
 with baubles

>   *Excellent for playing Kings & Queens. In the House of Lords the
>   number of baubles indicates the rank.*

Two Flapper dresses

>   *One was peach. We could see the little hand-sewn stitches. In those
>   days every village had a tailor & dressmaker.*

Bolts of cloth & lace collars

>   *Mother remembered Mr Snelgrove (Marshall & Snelgrove) coming
>   to the house from Oxord Street. The collars would be switched from
>   one dress to another.*

Wiltshire shepherd's smock
in heavy cream linen

>   *When we were older we recognised it as Gabriel Oak's in FAR FROM
>   THE MADDING CROWD. Gabriel deflating the bloated sheep.*

Little boy's scarlet jacket
with white braid

>   *The moths eventually got it.*

III

Flags & Headbands

The Engineer admits that the plethora of Union Jacks & England Flags has finally tested her patience: the Corsican *Testa Mora* is a small act of sabotage on Bastille Day and in the run up to the London Olympics. It looks great hanging from her bedroom window next to the neighbour's St George's Cross as I stroll with the Polymath to the Asian corner shop for milk & *Le Monde*. The emblem prisoner – head detached – is a timely reminder of the clearing of Moors from the Iberian Peninsula. And now she's telling us – slightly abashed by a gap where her tooth should be – how Pasquale Paoli adopted the flag in 1760 to continue the tradition of independence. *Freedom must walk by the torch of philosophy* he declared, re-styling the blindfold into a sporty headband.

Women & Men

It needs the solid knowledge of a soul
Who having lived and loved in woman's body
Has also lived and loved in the body of a man.

Ted Hughes, *Tales from Ovid* – 'Tiresias'

The Entrepreneur is blogging. Not about Nero's poor young slave Sporum – aka Sabina. She doesn't know about Pope Joan or the *Chronicon Pontificum et Imperatorum* and it's unlikely that Sandra does either. In any event Sandra isn't saying. She is choosing new hair. She removes her blond day wig, suddenly naked in her own shaved grey. She takes her time, gazing at the mannequins, fingering the soft filaments in her large & shapely hands. Little does she know that the Chevalier d'Eon was a male French diplomat & mistress to Louis Quinze – that he too spent the second half of his life as a woman. If she knew she might ask as Jupiter asks: *In their act of love, who takes the greater pleasure, man or woman?* On the other hand Sandra has chosen so presumably she does know. She has her sorrows but blindness is not one of them. And now she splashes out, popping both *Charlotte* and *Kaleigh* into her roomy bag.

Heads & Hats

The Polymath is wearing a straw hat to protect his head. He walks ahead, hands and fingers weaving a rhythm as he composes and conducts. For one who claims he cannot sing he brims with *poésies* that always sing to me. And even brimless hats can sing. The Art Dealer's bronze insignia once held a gemstone in its centre and was worn to ornament the red, yellow or purple turban atop a sheikh's noble head. Now the Polymath's saying that the Mexican Hat diagram represents the allowable states in the system and the height is the system's energy and – silly me! – the equilibrium state is the peak of the hat and the minima are just inside the rim in the form of a complete circle. But all I can see is the photo he took on our honeymoon: twenty-five men in sombreros on the back of a truck somewhere in Chihuahua.

Black Tie & Jacket

The Architect is wearing a black tie & jacket. Ariadne is sleeping her final sleep. But he did not abandon her. O he never would have abandoned her! Those years ago when she cut the thread and left him to his demons in the labyrinth … how he still watched out for her. Now we are gathered round him in a post-wake alert. He chooses *moules* followed by *coq au vin* and like a weather-vane the conversation changes to the Middle East.

Donkeys & Dreams

The old Berber re-appears like a mirage in the ochre landscape, jolting in a little cart behind his donkey. Earlier this morning, tramping the streets for a watercolour – *Vous connaissez Gallerie Almas?* – the rhythms of the women bewitched me. Then on impulse dashing for a train with the Polymath and here we are – held up at Ben Guerir! Dreaming under an ornamental tree, shaded from the midday sun as the old man disappears and men & boys enter & leave the *Salle de Prière.*

Through the train window, the mystical old man emerges from terracotta waves in the middle distance. At my side, in a canvas bag & bubble-wrap, a painting of two women in bright djellabas as they leave the Medina, holding a child's hand. Across the passage a sharp young Arab chats with the Polymath. Far in the distance, the speck of donkey & cart vanishes with the old man: *I have asked the embroiderers of Fez & Rabat to make a hammock for your dreams …*

Apitherapy

And thy Lord inspired the bee to build its cells in hills, on trees and in men's habitations. There issues from within their bodies a drink of varying colours, wherein is healing for men. AL-QUR'AN 16:68-69

I sit at my desk, face smeared in liquid gold, waiting for glucose oxydase to combine with my skin fluid and turn into hydrogen peroxide. Then it will slough necrotic tissue, speed up granulation and epithelialisation and heal my skin. The doctor pushes my hair from my face but his hand is not a healing hand. He has beautiful eyes but his steroids don't help and his penicillin has lost its efficacy. He's forgotten that a thousand years ago his ancestors trusted honey's anti-bacterial, anti-inflammatory and analgesic properties. My face is swollen, red and sore. He says that to find the floral source would be a wild goose chase but even Hippocrates knew: *honey cleans sores and ulcers of the lips, heals carbuncles and running sores.* It's lip-lickingly good. Delicious on toast, crackers and cake. The Polymath brings me milk and gingerbread. Then he remembers Plutarch. He shuts the window so I'm not a magnet. So I won't suffer the terrible fate of the poor young soldier Mithridates.

Glockenspiel & Cymbals

When the Architect shows me his painting of Beccles I search for a wherry with its horses & sails. Here's the church and the town and the River Bure. Then I see it. A little skiff with *Ariadne* daubed in red across the bow. But the boat was nameless when he'd sketched it *in situ*. So he'd returned home and perhaps it was Zerbinetta messing with his colours & brushes as he painted *Ariadne* to the sounds of glockenspiel & cymbals. Then the river-nymphs arrived with violins & cellos and he poured himself a glass of wine. He sat awhile to contemplate: the reflections on the river and questions of twilight – whether to add her constellation to the sky. Not so much concepts as echoes … And without even thinking *auf Naxos … os os.*

Football & Flu

The Engineer has picked up flu on the plane. But today's the first anniversary of that terrible day her father's mind was lost to her. Nothing will stop her. It's the first Home Match! She knits a scarf on the bus between Calvi & Bastia but its edges curl up and FORZA BASTIA disappears in a woolly chipolata. Oh but the ticket's a thing of beauty! Sad to say that fisticuffs, eyeballing & brawling in the benches stop the match. A throwback no doubt to the medieval mob dragging a pig's bladder to markers at each end of a town. Cicero notes that a man is killed while having a shave when an airfilled *follis* is lobbed into the barber's shop. On the twentieth anniversary of the Hillsborough disaster the Engineer lays a wreath of remembrance.

Cycles & Wheels

This week the Art Dealer is no longer certain that the insignia is exclusively Islamic. He needs to find the living Fibonacci of calendar history – one of the few souls alive who can spin and read off Metonic & Callipic cycles as Leonardo read sunflowers. So, as of yesterday he turns like a sunflower to the makers of Swiss watches and just one phone call to Geneva … I gaze up at the sky as I ride the old Berber's shoulders. He starts to spin and I stretch out my arms to the universe, imagine my mind the hub of a wheel, the spokes barely moving as the carriage gathers speed. I try to concentrate, to collect my thoughts into a single point of emptiness, for I've heard that only a vacant space can fill. Now, sitting in the single empty place on a bench in the John Betjeman Arms, St Pancras, I anticipate the Art Dealer. When he arrives he fills the recently-vacated gap next to me and orders a good bottle of Chilean red. We are so pleased to see each other we hardly notice the ebb and flow. Then he tells me that the space just below his kidney is occupied. Next week he will enter the Clinique St Paul for the nephrectomy.

L'Ochju di Santa Lucia

I'm wearing the pendant she brought back last time. She's off again at dawn. Not as Engineer. Not Director of Corsican Railways. She's going to 'scope out' potential sites on the border between the north and south, between Bastia and Calvi. She'll tread in the steps of Dorothy Carrington whose tales of vendettas on the granite island still captivate historians & travellers. The Engineer wants murders & mafia. She's creating an identikit for a feisty female Montalbano, integrating custom, dialect & history into her script. The medieval fishermen netting the sea snail *Astraea rugosa* are charmed like me by the seven spirals on its shell. They wear it for protection, calling it *L'Ochju di Santa Lucia.*

Bells & Minarets

The Art Dealer enjoys the shroud-shaped stones at the Church of Saint Mary and Saint Eanswythe in Folkestone. Only a short while later he is lying in his Paris apartment listening to the bells of Saint Leonard's in Hythe on the BBC. Now he is minded to visit the National Bell Museum near Toulouse. Maybe there he will discover a peel of thirteen. There's a minaret at Fez with thirteen plonks: a projectile spat out of a bird's beak to mark the thirteenth hour.

Grey Squirrels & Egyptian Geese

I'm papering the yellow wall with twelve sheets of music. There's a five bar intro and four concluding unsung bars. The white sheets face my window and mirror its shape. I sit at my desk pleased with the double aspect. To my right small gardens, rooftops & windows … a squirrel dancing along the fence. To my left a change of perspective.

It's like gazing at a lake – the red & black notes bobbing like crested grebes. As I approach, they attach themselves to words – *in clearings of trees* – and I think Chinese & /or Indonesian … That ancient scroll the Art Dealer rolled along the long teak table those years ago – *a vapour rises, spirals, lays thin blankets*. The notes like a melody in *slendro* … chimes & gongs of the gamelan … honks of Egyptian geese.

Nomads & Love Quests

Now I'm plastering walls with unpublished translations. I work like an artisan, plying a wash over lines of *terza rima*. The Prologue opens with a sun-burst of aureolin yellow, the eight tercets instantly revealing a rhythm of slightly varying breaths, the final single line rounding off the section but leaving it open, like a path with a stile. Two marginal glosses – emulated from The Rime of the Ancient Mariner – hover as I daub them in. The casual visitor might smile, surprised by the resemblance to financial bar graphs.

The old Berber enters the room. Neither historian nor meteorologist he is both palimpsest and weather-vane. He stands in the centre of the room, head cocked to the side. He doesn't move but I know he is crossing a stile. He closes his eyes, piercing through Dante and three written languages. He begins to hum then sits on the floor, lips pursed in a whisper. Soon he is singing, body rocking to the ancient customs that scroll before his inner eye – the nomads & love-quests, the weddings & deaths – fingers plucking the oud, voice now joyful now lamenting ...

أحبك أحبك أحبك يا حبيبي

Out-of-Roundness & Thin-walled Cylinders

When I look up there she is and I know he has died. Her face stands out pale against thick dark hair & winter coat. She's just off the train from Liverpool with a list of his early publications in *Proceedings of the Society for Experimental Stress Analysis, Vol. 13, No. 2, 1956.* I pay for her pint of Ghostship and when she cries her eyes are wide but her lips turned down & hands palm up like Giotto's *Lamentation.* She's followed in her father's profession so when tears flow I think of her dead Dad and think: *General Instability Pressure for Ring-Stiffened Cylinders* and pay for another Ghostship. She wrenches his autobiography from her backpack: 1950s B&Ws at MIT. 1980s Colour: little Engineer on the Professor's lap. Little Engineer smiling with her drop-dead mother. How it all makes sense – those *Effects of Boundary Conditions and Initial Out-of-Roundness on the Strength of Thin-Walled Cylinders.* And when I read the FB posts (outbursts. anger. crying. fear. high-IQ. exposure. anxiety. that she identifies on the online *GENDER & AUTISM GRID*) all that comes to mind is *Gravity & Grace.*

IV

Requiem for the Engineer

i.m. Dr Diana Archer Galletly – 1974-2014

Blood Letting

I

The Engineer says the priest came to hear her confession but she couldn't think of anything terrible she'd done. [The dialyzer is the key to haemodialysis.] She is tearful & apologetic. Calls herself *grouchy mess* & *hysterical witch*. She's so wired-up that the 'ports' look like multi-coloured hair bobbins. [The average person has 10 to 12 pints of blood; during dialysis only one pint (about two cups) is outside the body at a time.] I collect up phone, cards & photo of L. Follow her bed out of the HDU back to the ICU. Sometimes her large brown eyes seem to rest on me.

II

Sometimes her brown eyes settle on me. Like a butterfly on my skin. Her hair is feather-soft. She complains it hasn't been washed. [There are two sections in the dialyzer; the section for dialysate and the section for blood.] The nutritionist asks what she likes to eat. *Anything Mediterranean.* Then removes the untouched sausage & mash. [The two sections are divided by a semi-permeable membrane so they don't mix together.] I hold the Engineer's hand. We look at the photo of L. Fifteen & sitting her mocks.

III

Other times her eyes are eloquent. Large white rather than brimstone yellow. The nurse explains why she keeps being moved between IC & HD. Her washed hair fans out dark against the pillow. [The dialysis solution is then flushed down the drain along with the waste.] We talk about medieval blood letting – she almost laughs. Doctors optimistic but. Stress situation might change & suddenly.

IV

Nor butterfly nor Engineer. Eyes barely slits in *setae*. No more to flit from iPhone to photo. Never to rest on me. Nor blood nor dialysate – the machines are silent, pushed aside. Her head seems slighter, hair curtained against her face, lips a little parted. One cold hand grips an olive wood cross. As I lean to kiss her brow, it's as if she chose to speak … *For, if I imp my wing on thine, affliction shall advance the flight in me.*

Soil & Grit

I am superimposing images onto my poem. I begin with CHAEMELON by Leonhart Fuchs. I print the illustration on tracing paper and place it on top of the poem. In a second attempt – using photo-fix – I stretch the herb so it lies over the poem, as if wrenched from your small Corsican garden and left on my prose poem table, still pungent with rain, soil & grit. The flower-heads reach up through the title and the roots dangle down below the last line. Last night I coloured each little stigma yellow, leaving the petals white. The word camillon is just discernible between two lines. I cut out my name from David Jones' lettering – copied from my mother's *ANATHÉMATA FABERSON DINIVM* and spelt the French way. This morning I've shown it to the Polymath. As you know, he doesn't believe in an after-life, but he misses you ... which is like sending his love anyway.

Sage & Water

I keep fading & fading the image but still the poem won't show
through. All I can see is the SALVIA from your garden, you stand-
ing at our door with your arms full. Now suddenly this flashback to
the Polymath's darkroom, tense with excitement as the image first began
to emerge through water. So I print the poem in bold and place the
wild sage underneath. Then print on soft grey Ingres Pastel Paper 90g/
m^2. Next I arrange it in a black frame and step back. It's SALVIA semi-
submerged in water. Ophelia singing as she floats down-river.

Body & Wings

I try using a photo from your portfolio but the leaves are too lush. Their deep dark green and the dense cluster of florets obscure everything else. Ah, but you'd love this Leonhart Fuchs. You would tense with the precision – pinning it to the poem like a rare insect, a piece of jewellery, a brooch to be worn on special occasions (first your mother's funeral, then your father's): LANTANA. Colouring the three flower heads highlights the impression of insect – antennae & head erect above body, wings & tail. I hang it on the wall, step back to view at a distance. Now it's a headstone, the dark engraving in cruciform.

Crossbill & Fruit

The bird arrives with a scent of firs & pines. I like to think it's bringing the produce of your garden. Apricot. Grapefruit. Olive. The Benedictine monk sketched this finch – *a little bigger than Larks* – untinted in 1251. Now it alights on my poem, berry in its wide-open beak. I jiggle its head under 'Engineer'. Finally in place, feet above *Alaudis parum majores*, I can fancy it perched on my Turkish birdbath, striking *one point upon the other, so as to show the transverse sickles.* At a distance the bird appears veiled by words – hints of old proverbs – and folklore tells how it got its beak wrenching the nails from Jesus' hands and feet.

Collaging the Bohemian Angels

I

He arrives vertical. Hovers over 'Absence' so I ask if one absence is equal to another? Is weightlessness weighed by pressure of? ANDELIK is suspended in music. Now he is here for your mother, lingers as I re-play you singing at the funeral in Liverpool. *Pie Jesu.* Your beautiful soprano. ANDELIK illuminated on parchment – strange that I scroll through the manuscript to make you a gift. But it's too easy to place a large tracing above or under the poem. I must struggle with the angel. Work in miniature. Shrink him.

II

Every Angel is terrible. How to print on thin blue tissue to emphasise the wings as he hovers over *Pie Jesu*? If I should tear the tissue – that dream of long-tailed tits fluttering & cheeping, trusting me in their tilted nest – I might injure ecstasy. The tune plays faintly through the blue, faint music from Fauré's *Requiem* on plain tissue cut with scissors. Outside, the sun you loved blazes in a cloudless sky. I tried to work that night in the silence, feet bare like the angel's. Now I gaze at the picture for hours. The music's slipping, crimpling softly behind the blue-winged figure.

III

Almost a girl – this figure in a green robe. ANDELIK plays his lute which appears weightless as his animated hands & fingers pluck the strings. His eyes are turned aside, large and childlike, stilled by harmony. Like an angel you mastered the violin, your playing so mellifluous that a sleeping neighbour thought it a visitation. O girl, you with your pale, cool hands arcing the bow, dancing the fingerboard. O fractal-angel of your own design, how can I capture your complexity? No mathematician, I'll cut up ANDELIK – construct a puzzle of disparate pieces. His face yours. *A girl almost.*

IV

Is it sacrilege? Is this hesitance before the incision my answer? The tip of the scissorblade pricks through the tracing like a jet of breath. Will the two heads on the table meet in a new cohesion, the lute & harp as mirrored halves, the blue, green & orange of ANDELIK's robes colours of the fruits from yours and Rilke's gardens? So risky it's silly to attempt? I go in trepidation – the wedding dress you hand-sewed exchanged for the angel's gown. And look, there are four hands – subliminal music in the mind. There's a gap where the halo was … O I can see that witty sparkle in your eyes!

V

To enjoy this reconfiguration requires faith. To sever a medieval head and replace it with yours: one false cut and I must begin the process again. The halo rocks on the table – sickle moon. I scissor you out of your wedding dress, paste you into the green gown. Your new hands and fingers pluck the lute strings with conviction and it's time to include the harpist, discreetly, from the wings. The blue robe seeps in like a water-colourist's wash as I release the long curl of your hair, place the whole on a backdrop of orange. The picture comes to life. Two shadow hands strum a harp. Your face is radiant – illuminated under an arch.

VI

No longer shocking – as if with typical passion you adjust to multiplicity with ease. The harp equal to your body, to the *size* of you – your many arts vibrating through a single string. The lyre held playfully aside, just another piece of the puzzle that fits. That twirl of hair's still dangling and I know I could add the lute – you with your three pairs of hands! But no, I won't intrude. You look so happy & relaxed as if you've truly found your music. O tell me Angel in a blue robe – how did the halo transform into a plumed fascinator?

Impact Under Pressure (I)

No more is it your dread of a strong wind off the sea: this approach through the mountains so as not to over-run the runway. The 'mountain in the sea' crowds at our windows, the tilted wings perilously tipping earth – fifty million years of sedimentary rock pressed against granite. Now the devastation at your flat: specialist computer equipment, dictionaries & *Teach Yourself* Czech, Corse & Gaelic; football regalia, violin & guitar, photos of L. Books & more books: *Guide de la Flore en Corse, Papillons de Méditerranée, The Geometry of Pasta* and shelves of maths, physics and *Structural Engineering* in French & English. In a bottom drawer, academic documents & awards. On your bed, cuddly tigers crushed in a heap.

Impact Under Pressure (II)

I know I'll get bitten, standing in the wilderness of your garden contemplating the ruins of saplings you planted. Apricot. Grapefruit. Olive. Heat & insects penetrate & invade. Is it clichéd to equate my flesh with fruit? I don't wish infection but can't desist – standing skin exposed in the brittle scrub & gangly weeds, eye irritants on the breeze. Later, walking back into Calvi, I'm riveted by a fossil preserved in a block of feldspar. *Fern, Fougère, Filetta*: Corsican emblem & symbol of the people – so well-embedded it's impossible to uproot.

Impact Under Pressure (III)

*L*armes, *lácrime, lacrimae:* composed of water, salts, antibodies & antibacterial enzymes. All that dust in your flat, allergens in the garden! You arrive – via Cambridge, Marseilles, Calvi – at La Chapelle Sainte Loretta, coffin draped with a flag – the *Testa Mora* that once goaded Cambridge neighbours, and scarves – SC Bastia & Liverpool FC. The priest sings a *Corse lamentu*, gestures to lay our hands where you are laid, and all that's suppressed is released in a stream of protein-based hormones – prolactin, adrenocorticotropic & leucine enkephalin (a natural pain-killer).

Impact Under Pressure (IV)

The coffin is pushed into what resembles a left-luggage locker on the mountain. André bricks up and seals the lid with the cement he mixes *in situ*, then stands aside and sings an ancient lament. In a gale of howling pines we climb the stony track to the 11th century Notre Dame de la Serra, wind tearing at scarves & hair. O blue moon earring! O mother-of-pearl & silver! O vanished sickle moon! My mother's gift to me, lost in the earth – and as I glance one last time at your name & dates (1974–2014), it's as if you had opened my eyes. That fossil near your flat, that Tyrrhenian wall lizard at Saleccia. Now it slips between fern & rock – to be compressed in strata.

Impact Under Pressure (V)

You followed Dorothy Carrington – her donkeys & mules – in search of histories, recipes, folklore & song. Now we follow you, changing trains at Ponteleccia to roll through panoramas of mountains & canyons: oleander, forests of sweet chestnut, hairpin bends & precipitous drops, tunnels hacked out of rock. Suddenly the driver slams on the brakes and blares his horn! A massive black *sanglier* is running for its life, caught between tons of hurtling metal and the vertical face of rock. I imagine its panicked eyes and battering heart – echoes of Moose & gasoline! Will it escape or be crushed into granite, embossed in bone & blood?

Impact Under Pressure (VI)

As Jean-Claude Acquaviva sings his lead and the packed nave tingles palpably, I recall your joy when he offered you his tuition. The cathedral resounds with a *lamentu* and my skin prickles. *A Filetta* : six men in close formation, one hand curled to an ear, the other raised in a gesture of beckon & wave. They sing of love & death, land & animal, bandit, war & independence, now leaning in, arms around shoulders, now crouching body to body, ear to ear. Later, as we begin our descent from the Citadel, stumbling on ancient paving lit by the moon & stars, music pierces the stillness and I glance at a window. Four men are singing round a kitchen table as a dark-haired woman looks on, leaning against the door.

V

Rings & Circles

I

The Polymath holds a pencil in his right hand and a blue pen in his left. The eraser sits next to his spec case and empty Virgin coffee cup. Red, black & green sway in the little office of his jacket pocket and his specs hang low on his nose. In his long fingers the pencil hovers above his diagram like an artist's brush, a conductor's baton measuring time as the train speeds to Aberdeen. The blue pen doubles as a ruler, guiding the dodecahedron through its many metamorphoses. The pencil swoops, inserting dotted rings & semi-circles, arrows, darts & chevrons onto the model – these analogies of space and time across physical and biological structures. He calls it a Model of the Mind and I'm minded of those wondrous childhood atlases that made the earth come alive mapping the great migrations of the natural world – flocks of swans & geese darkening the North American skies, herds of zebra, gazelles & wildebeest traversing the great savannahs of Africa, shoals of whales & turtles plying the oceans of the globe.

II

The Art Dealer is travelling too, his spirit fired by a timely opportunity in Hong Kong where for once he has the money and, he says, even if the world continues its meltdown, will be able to put food on the table and pay the rent. He sends me a jpeg and I fall in love with the thirteen horses. It's an incense-burning altar, unearthed in an excavated tumulus, entering the collections of the tzar in 1716 and now preserved in the Hermitage Museum, St. Petersburg. I carry it in my head on the ferries to the Northern Isles, to Orkney's neolithic village at Skara Brae, to the circular chambered tomb at Maeshowe, the standing stones at Stenness. I stand in the middle of the Ring of Brodgar, the lochs – once marshland – and surrounding hills glowing in the early sunset. Suddenly the thirty-six still-existing stones transform into thirteen horses cantering round the central hearth. Then, just as abruptly, they turn and gallop away, manes flying, hooves thundering as they begin their return to the great Russian steppes of 2500 B.C.E.

Notes

SECTION I

Mules & Men

– the quote is from *Islamic Slaves* by M A Khan, Internet 2011.

SECTION II

The Diarists

In 2014, in a collaboration between the Scott Polar Research Institute, Cambridge and *PN Review*, eight Cambridge-based poets were each commissioned to write a poem inspired by an object of their choice from the permanent display in the Museum. At the time, I was privileged to be working with a 'diarist' whose father had been an eminent explorer. Like Scott he belonged to the period in Britain before the First World War, when there was still a sense of expanding horizons. Both men were compulsive adventurers, Scott as a naval man from the age of fourteen, Alexander Wollaston, known as Sandy, as a medical doctor, botanist and entomologist. Both were diarists, but whereas Scott's final expedition was to Antarctica 1910-1913, Wollaston wrote about his experiences with the British New Guinea Expedition 1910-1912. Like Scott he'd narrowly missed death on numerous occasions, but unlike Scott, his tragic death at King's College Cambridge had nothing to do with his expeditions. So, to my chosen 'object' of letters and diaries on display in the Museum, I added the letters and diaries of Wollaston and the biography by his late son Nicholas Wollaston. The former had been compiled and edited by the 'Diarist's' mother and were published in 1933 by Cambridge University Press. The sequence is an attempt to amalgamate facts and quotes from these texts with the stories, memories and conversations Georgina Thompson generously shared throughout our four years working together.

Ice & Tears

– the first quote is from *The Last Letters*, edited by Heather Lane, Naomi Boneham and Robert D Smith; published by The Scott Polar Research Institute, Cambridge 2012. The second is from *Letters and Diaries of A.F.R. Wollaston,* edited by Mary Wollaston, Cambridge University Press 1933, p261 and *My Father Sandy,* by Nicholas Wollaston, Short Books 2003, p188.

Penguin & Lamb

– the quotes are from *Journals Captain Scott's Last Expedition*, Oxford World Classics 2006.

Glaciers & Robins

– the epigraph is from *The Worst Journey in the World* by Apsley Cherry-Garrard, CPSIA United States.

Small Differences in the Spectrum of Black – the quote is from Jonathan Swift's *Gulliver's Travels*.

De Incidentibus in Fluido / Hecest Horrenda Caribdis

– the quote is from Samuel Coleridge's *The Rime of the Ancient Mariner*.

Notes & Quotes

– the information in this poem is adapted from texts in the display cabinets at the Scott Polar Museum, Cambridge.

Crocodiles & Frigate Birds

– the canoe is in the Museum of Archeology & Anthropology, Cambridge.

Bedtime Stories

– the quotes are from *Letters and Diaries of A.F.R. Wollaston* and *My Father Sandy*.

Papuan Canoes & Items (Property of the Royal Geographical Society) Lost Overboard

– the italicised names are Papuan and the bracketed their translations; these, together with the items lost and the asterisked note, are from *Letters and Diaries of A.F.R. Wollaston* pp 124-5 & 149-50 respectively.

Section III

Heads & Hats

– refers to the Mexican hat diagram in cosmology.

Glockenspiel & Cymbals

— the poem alludes to Richard Strauss's opera *Ariadne auf Naxos*.

Nomads & Love Quests

– the Arabic quote means 'I love you, I love you, I love you.'

Section IV

Soil & Grit

– this and the following two poems refer to the German physician and botanist Leonhart Fuchs. His chief renown is as the author of a large book about plants and their uses as medicines, i.e. a Herbal Book. It was first published in 1542 in Latin.

Crossbill & Fruit

– the Benedictine monk referred to is Matthew Paris (c.1200-1259), an artist in illustrated manuscripts and cartographer based at St Alban's Abbey in Hertfordshire.

Collaging the Bohemian Angels

– this sequence refers to *The Passional of Abbes Kunigunde*, an illuminated Latin manuscript commissioned by Prague Benedictine Abbes Kunigunde of Bohemia, daughter of King Ottokar II of Bohemia after 1312. The work was written and possibly also illuminated by Prague canon Beneš, who served as a priest in the St George's Convent.

Impact Under Pressure

– the title of this sequence refers to the autobiography of the same title by Diana Galletly's late father, Professor Gerrard Duncan Galletly (1928–2013).

Impact Under Pressure VI

– Jean Claude Acquaviva is the lead singer of the internationally-renowned Corsican polyphonic choral group, A Filetta.